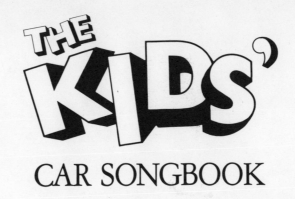

# CAR SONGBOOK

# CAR SONGBOOK

Compiled by Gary Delfiner

Running Press
Philadelphia, Pennsylvania

Canadian representatives: General Publishing Co.,Ltd. 30 Lesmill Road, Don Mills, Ontario M3B 2T6. International representatives: Worldwide Media Services, Inc., 115 East 23rd Street, New York, NY 10010.

ISBN 0-89471-602-6 (paper)
ISBN 0-89471-603-4 (library binding)
ISBN 0-89471-604-2 (package)

This book may be ordered by mail from the publisher. Please include $1.00 postage. **But try your bookstore first!** Running Press Book Publishers, 125 South Twenty-second Street, Philadelphia, Pennsylvania 19103.

Cover design by Toby Schmidt
Cover illustration by Linda Gist
Interior illustrations by Deirdre Newman Griffin
Typography: Garamond by rci, Philadelphia, PA; Helvetica Condensed Shaded by Letraset
Printed by South Sea International, Ltd., Hong Kong

Dedicated to my aunt, my teacher,
Anna-Mae Edell

# Contents

Each of the songs in this book is a classic, sung by kids in cars, at camp, just about anywhere kids are found.

Four favorites that seem to come up during every sing-along are ''Frère Jacques,'' ''Frog, He Went A-Courting,'' ''This Old Man,'' and ''Twinkle, Twinkle, Little Star.'' Because no compilation of kids' songs is truly complete without these, we've reprinted them from our own *Family Car Songbook*.

For more sing-along fun, *The Family Car Songbook* is available as a book or as a book and audiocassette package.

# Old MacDonald Had a Farm

Old MacDonald had a
    farm, E - I - E - I - O
And on his farm he had a
    cat, E - I - E - I - O
With a mew-mew here
    and a mew-mew there
Here a mew, there a mew,
    ev'rywhere a mew-mew
Old MacDonald had a
    farm, E - I - E - I - O

Old MacDonald had a
    farm, E - I - E - I - O
And on his farm he had a
    pig, E - I - E - I - O

With an oink-oink here
    and an oink-oink there
Here an oink, there an
    oink, ev'rywhere an
    oink-oink
Old MacDonald had a
    farm, E - I - E - I - O

Old MacDonald had a
    farm, E - I - E - I - O
And on his farm he had a
    duck, E - I - E - I - O
With a quack-quack here
    and a quack-quack there
Here a quack, there a
    quack, ev'rywhere a
    quack-quack
Old MacDonald had a
    farm, E - I - E - I - O

Old MacDonald had a
    farm, E - I - E - I - O
And on his farm he had a

cow, E - I - E - I - O
With a moo-moo here and
a moo- moo there
Here a moo, there a moo,
ev'rywhere a moo-moo
Old MacDonald had a
farm, E - I - E - I - O

Old MacDonald had a
farm, E - I - E - I - O

And on his farm he had a
mule, E - I - E - I - O
With a hee-haw here and a
hee- haw there
Here a hee, there a haw,
ev'rywhere a hee-haw
Old MacDonald had a
farm, E - I - E - I - O

Old MacDonald had a

farm, E - I - E - I - O
And on his farm he had
some chicks,
E - I - E - I - O
With a chick-chick here
and a chick-chick
there
Here a chick, there a chick,
ev'rywhere a chick-chick
Old MacDonald had a
farm, E - I - E - I - O

# Twinkle, Twinkle, Little Star

Twinkle, twinkle, little star
How I wonder what you
    are!
Up above the world so high
Like a diamond in the sky.

Twinkle, twinkle, little star
How I wonder what you
    are!

When the blazing sun goes
    down
Darkness falls all over town.

Then you show your tiny
    light
Twinkling, twinkling
through the night.

Twinkle, twinkle, little star

How I wonder what you
    are!

Weary travelers in the dark
Thank you for your little
    spark
Who could see which path
    to go
If you did not twinkle so?

Twinkle, twinkle, little star
How I wonder what you
    are!

In the dark sky you remain
Peeking through the
    windowpane
And you never shut your
    eye
'Til the sun is in the sky.

▫

Twinkle, twinkle, little star

How I wonder what you
    are!

▫

As your bright and tiny
    spark
Lights the traveler in the
    dark

Though I know not what
    you are
Twinkle, twinkle, little star!

▫

Twinkle, twinkle, little star
How I wonder what you
    are!

# Bingo

There was a man had a dog,
And Bingo was his name, O!
B-I-N-G-O, B-I-N-G-O,
B-I-N-G-O,
And Bingo was his name, O!

# Three Blind Mice

*May be sung as a round.*

Three blind mice, three
   blind mice
See how they run! See how
   they run!
They all ran after the
   farmer's wife

Who cut off their tails
   with a carving
   knife
Did you ever hear such a
   tale in your life
As three blind mice!

# Mary Had a Little Lamb

Mary had a little lamb,
    little lamb, little lamb
Mary had a little lamb
Its fleece was white as snow
And ev'rywhere that
    Mary went, Mary went,
    Mary went
And ev'rywhere that
    Mary went
The lamb was sure to go
He followed her to school
    one day, school one day,
    school one day
He followed her to school
    one day

That was against the rule
It made the children laugh
    and play, laugh and
    play, laugh and play
It made the children laugh
    and play
To see a lamb at school

So the Teacher turned him
    out, turned him out,
    turned him out
So the Teacher turned him
    out
But still he lingered near
And waited patiently
    about, -ly about,
    -ly about
And waited patiently about
Till Mary did appear
And then he ran to her
    and laid, her and laid,
    her and laid
And then he ran to her

and laid
His head upon her arm
As if he said "I'm not
    afraid, not afraid, not
    afraid"
As if he said "I'm not
    afraid
You'll keep me from all
    harm."
    ▫

"What makes the lamb
love Mary so, Mary so,
Mary so?"
"What makes the lamb
    love Mary so?"
The eager children cry
"O, Mary loves the lamb
    you know, lamb you
    know, lamb you know
O, Mary loves the lamb
    you know,"
The Teacher did reply

"And you each gentle
    animal, animal, animal
And you each gentle
    animal
In confidence may bind
And make them follow at
    your call, at your call,
    at your call
And make them follow at
    your call
If you are always kind."

# My Bonnie Lies Over the Ocean

My bonnie lies over the
  ocean
My bonnie lies over the sea
My bonnie lies over the
  ocean
Oh, bring back my bonnie
  to me!

Bring back, bring back
Oh, bring back my bonnie
  to me, to me!
Bring back, bring back
Oh, bring back my bonnie
  to me, to me!

Oh, blow ye winds over the
  ocean
Oh, blow ye winds over the
  sea
Oh, blow ye winds over the
  ocean
And bring back my bonnie
  to me.

Bring back, bring back
Oh, bring back my bonnie
  to me, to me!
Bring back, bring back
Oh, bring back my bonnie
  to me, to me!

Last night when in bed I
  lay dreaming
Last night when the moon
  was on high
Last night when in bed I
  lay sleeping

I thought I heard dear
  bonnie cry.

🔲

Bring back, bring back
Oh, bring back my bonnie
  to me, to me!
Bring back, bring back
Oh, bring back my bonnie
  to me, to me!

🔲

My bonnie was sleeping so
soundly
My bonnie was sleeping so
tight
My bonnie was sleeping so
soundly
In his little crib painted
white.

🔲

Bring back, bring back
Oh, bring back my bonnie
  to me, to me!
Bring back, bring back

Oh, bring back my bonnie
  to me to me!

🔲

The winds, they blew over
  the ocean
The winds, they blew over
  the sea
The winds, they blew over
  the ocean
And brought back my
  bonnie to me, to me
And brought back my
  bonnie to me.

# Baa, Baa, Black Sheep

"Baa! Baa! Black sheep,
   have you any wool?"
"Yes, kind sir, I've three
   bags full
One for my master, and
   one for my dame
And one for the little boy
   who lives down the
   lane."

"Can you weave three
   blankets for his bed?"
"Yes, to reach from toe to
   head
One for his cradle, and
   one, soft and warm
And one to keep him
   tucked in, safe from
   harm."

# Ring Around a Rosie

Ring around a rosie
A pocket full of posies
Slowly, slowly, all fall down

# The Farmer in the Dell

The farmer in the dell
The farmer in the dell
Hi-ho, the derry-o
The farmer in the dell

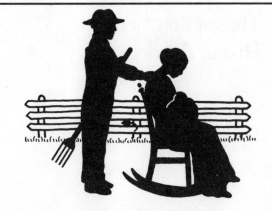

The farmer in the dell

The farmer takes a wife

The farmer takes a wife
Hi-ho, the derry-o
The farmer takes a wife

The wife takes a child
The wife takes a child

Hi-ho, the derry-o
The wife takes a child

The child takes a nurse
The child takes a nurse
Hi-ho, the derry-o
The child takes a nurse

The nurse takes a dog
The nurse takes a dog
Hi-ho, the derry-o

The nurse takes a dog

The dog takes a cat
The dog takes a cat
Hi-ho, the derry-o
The dog takes a cat

The cat takes a rat
The cat takes a rat
Hi-ho, the derry-o

The cat takes a rat

The rat takes a cheese
The rat takes a cheese
Hi-ho, the derry-o
The rat takes a cheese

The cheese stands alone
The cheese stands alone
Hi-ho, the derry-o
The cheese stands alone

# Oh Where, Oh Where Has My Little Dog Gone?

Oh where, oh where has
    my little dog gone
Oh where, oh where can
    he be?

With his ears cut short and
    his tail cut long
Oh where, oh where is
    he?

# John Jacob Jingleheimer Schmidt

John Jacob Jingleheimer
    Schmidt
His name is my name too
Whenever we go out the

people like to shout:
"John Jacob Jingleheimer
    Schmidt"
Tra la la la la la la

# Alouette

Alouette gentille alouette
Alouette je te plumerai
Je te plumerai la tête
Je te plumerai la tête
Et la tête, et la tête
Et la tête, et la tête
Alouette gentille alouette
Alouette je te plumerai

Alouette gentille alouette
Alouette je te plumerai
Je te plumerai le bec
Je te plumerai le bec
Et la tête, et la tête
Et la tête, et la tête
Alouette gentille alouette
Alouette je te plumerai

# The Bear Goes Over the Mountain

The bear goes over the
   mountain, the bear goes
   over the mountain
The bear goes over the
   mountain, to see what
   he could see
To see what he could see,

   to see what he could see
But the other side of the
   mountain, the other side
   of the mountain
The other side of the
   mountain is all that he
   could see.

# The Star Spangled Banner

O say can you see by the
  dawn's early light
What so proudly we hail'd
  at the twilight's last
  gleaming
Whose broad stripes and
  bright stars through the
  perilous fight
O'er the ramparts we
  watch'd, were so
  gallantly streaming?
And the rocket's red glare,
  the bombs bursting
  in air
Gave proof through the

night that our flag was
  still there
O say does that star
  spangled banner
  yet wave
O'er the land of the free
  and the home of the
  brave?

On the shore dimly seen
  through the mists of
  the deep
Where the foe's haughty
  host in dread silence
  reposes
What is that which the
  breeze, o'er the towering
  steep
As it fitfully blows, half
  conceals, half discloses?
Now it catches the gleam
  of the morning's first
  beam
In full glory reflected now

shines in the stream
'Tis the star spangled
banner—O long may it
wave
O'er the land of the free
and the home of the
brave!

□

And where is that band
who so vauntingly swore
The havoc of war and the
battle's confusion
A home and a Country
should leave us no
more?
Their blood has wash'd out
their foul footstep's
pollution.
No refuge could save the
hireling and slave
From the terror of flight or
the gloom of the grave
And the star spangled
banner in triumph doth
wave
O'er the land of the free
and the home of the
brave.

□

O thus be it ever when
freemen shall stand
Between their lov'd home
and the war's desolation!
Blest with vict'ry and peace
may the heav'n rescued
land
Praise the power that hath
made and preserv'd us a
nation!
Then conquer we must,
when our cause it is just
And this be our
motto—''In God is
our Trust,''
And the star spangled
banner in triumph shall
wave
O'er the land of the free
and the home of the
brave.

# Itsy Bitsy Spider

The itsy bitsy spider went
   up the waterspout
Down came the rain and
   washed the spider out

Out came the sun and
   dried up all the rain
Now itsy bitsy spider goes
   up the spout again

# Sing a Song of Sixpence

Sing a song of sixpence
A pocket full of rye
Four and twenty blackbirds
Baked in a pie
When the pie was open'd
The birds began to sing
Oh, wasn't that a dainty
    dish
To set before the King?

The King was in his

counting-house
Counting out his money
The Queen was in the
    parlor
Eating bread and honey
The Maid was in the
    garden
Hanging out the clothes
There came a little
    blackbird
And kissed her on the
    nose

# The Muffin Man

Oh, have you met the
   Muffin Man
The Muffin Man, the
   Muffin Man
Oh, have you met the
   Muffin Man
Who lives in Drury Lane?

Oh, yes we've met the
   Muffin Man
The Muffin Man, the
   Muffin Man
Oh, yes we've met the
   Muffin Man
Who lives in Drury Lane!

28

# Oh Dear, What Can the Matter Be?

Oh, dear, what can the
matter be?
My dear, what can the
matter be?
My dear, what can the
matter be?
Johnny's too long at the
fair.

♪

He promised he'd buy me
a fairing should please
me
And then for a kiss, Oh! he
vowed he would tease me

He promised to buy me a
bunch of blue ribbons
To tie up my lovely brown
hair. And it's

♪

Oh, dear, what can the
matter be?

My dear, what can the
matter be?
My dear, what can the
matter be?
Johnny's too long at the
fair.

♪

He promised he'd bring
me a big bunch of posies
A garland of lilies, a
garland of roses
A little straw hat, to set off
the blue ribbons

That tie up my lovely
    brown hair. And it's

Oh, dear, what can the
    matter be?

My dear, what can the
    matter be?
My dear, what can the
    matter be?
Johnny's too long at the
    fair.

# I'm a Little Teapot

I'm a little teapot, short
    and stout
Here's my handle, here's
    my spout

When I get all steamed up,
    hear me shout
"Lift me up and pour me
    out!"

# Frog, He Went A-Courting

Frog, he went a-courting,
   and he did ride
Unh-hunh, unh-hunh
Frog, he went a-courting,
   and he did ride
Unh-hunh, unh-hunh
Frog, he went a-courting,
   and he did ride
With sword and pistol by
   his side
Unh-hunh, unh-hunh,
   unh-hunh

He bridled and saddled a

big striped snail
Unh-hunh, unh-hunh
He bridled and saddled a
   big striped snail
Unh-hunh, unh-hunh
He bridled and saddled a
   big striped snail
And rode it 'tween the

horns and tail
Unh-hunh, unh-hunh,
   unh-hunh

Rode the snail to Miss
   Mouse's door
Unh-hunh, unh-hunh
Rode the snail to Miss
   Mouse's door
Unh-hunh, unh-hunh
Rode the snail to Miss
   Mouse's door
Where he had often been

before
Unh-hunh, unh-hunh,
   unh-hunh

He called, "Miss Mouse,
   are you within?"
Unh-hunh, unh-hunh
He called, "Miss Mouse,
   are you within?"
Unh-hunh, unh-hunh
He called, "Miss Mouse,
   are you within?"
"Yes, sir, for I'm sitting
   down to spin."
Unh-hunh, unh-hunh,
   unh-hunh

Frog, he took Miss Mouse
   upon his knee
Unh-hunh, unh-hunh
Frog, he took Miss Mouse
   upon his knee
Unh-hunh, unh-hunh
Frog, he took Miss Mouse
   upon his knee
And asked, "My dear, will
   you marry me?"
Unh-hunh, unh-hunh,
   unh-hunh

"Why, without my Uncle
   Rat's consent
Unh-hunh, unh-hunh

"Why, without my Uncle
   Rat's consent
Unh-hunh, unh-hunh
"Why, without my Uncle
   Rat's consent
I'd not marry e'en the
   president."
Unh-hunh, unh-hunh,
   unh-hunh

Frog jumped on his snail
   and rode away
Unh-hunh, unh-hunh
Frog jumped on his snail
   and rode away
Unh-hunh, unh-hunh

Frog jumped on his snail
and rode away
Vowed to come back
another day
Unh-hunh, unh-hunh,
unh-hunh

Now Uncle Rat, when he
came home
Unh-hunh, unh-hunh
Now Uncle Rat, when he
came home
Unh-hunh, unh-hunh
Now Uncle Rat, when he
came home
Asked, "Who's been here
since I was gone?"
Unh-hunh, unh-hunh,
unh-hunh

"A very fine frog's been
calling here
Unh-hunh, unh-hunh
"A very fine frog's been
calling here
Unh-hunh, unh-hunh
"A very fine frog's been
calling here
And asked me for to be his
dear."
Unh-hunh, unh-hunh,
unh-hunh

Uncle Rat, he laughed and
shook his sides
Unh-hunh, unh-hunh
Uncle Rat, he laughed and
shook his sides
Unh-hunh, unh-hunh
Uncle Rat, he laughed and
shook his sides
To think his niece would be
a bride
Unh-hunh, unh-hunh,
unh-hunh

So Uncle Rat, he rode to
town
Unh-hunh, unh-hunh

So Uncle Rat, he rode to
    town
Unh-hunh, unh-hunh
So Uncle Rat, he rode to
    town
To buy Miss Mouse a
    wedding gown
Unh-hunh, unh-hunh,
    unh-hunh

□

Say where the wedding
    supper shall be
Unh-hunh, unh-hunh
Say where the wedding
    supper shall be
Unh-hunh, unh-hunh

Say where the wedding
    supper shall be
Down by the river in a
    hollow tree
Unh-hunh, unh-hunh,
    unh-hunh

□

Say what the wedding
    supper shall be
Unh-hunh, unh-hunh
Say what the wedding
    supper shall be
Unh-hunh, unh-hunh
Say what the wedding
    supper shall be
One green bean and a

black-eyed pea
Unh-hunh, unh-hunh,
    unh-hunh

□

Tell us, how was Miss
    Mousie dressed
Unh-hunh, unh-hunh
Tell us, how was Miss
    Mousie dressed
Unh-hunh, unh-hunh
Tell us, how was Miss
    Mousie dressed
In a cobweb veil and her
    Sunday best
Unh-hunh, unh-hunh,
    unh-hunh

Tell us next, what the Frog
  did wear
Unh-hunh, unh-hunh
Tell us next, what the Frog
  did wear
Unh-hunh, unh-hunh
Tell us next, what the Frog
  did wear
Sky-blue pants and a
  doublet fair
Unh-hunh, unh-hunh,
  unh-hunh

◻

The first guest to call was
  the bumblebee
Unh-hunh, unh-hunh

The first guest to call was
  the bumblebee
Unh-hunh, unh-hunh
The first guest to call was
  the bumblebee
And played them a fiddle
  upon his knee
Unh-hunh, unh-hunh,
  unh-hunh

◻

The next to come were the
  duck and drake
Unh-hunh, unh-hunh
The next to come were the
  duck and drake
Unh-hunh, unh-hunh

The next to come were the
  duck and drake
Who ate every crumb of
  the wedding cake
Unh-hunh, unh-hunh,
  unh-hunh

◻

"Come now, Mrs. Mouse,
  may we have some beer
Unh-hunh, unh-hunh
"Come now, Mrs. Mouse,
  may we have some beer
Unh-hunh, unh-hunh
"Come now, Mrs. Mouse,
  may we have some beer
That your uncle and I may

have some cheer?''
Unh-hunh, unh-hunh,
    unh-hunh


"Pray, Mr. Frog, will you
    give us a song
Unh-hunh, unh-hunh
"Pray, Mr. Frog, will you
    give us a song
Unh-hunh, unh-hunh
"Pray, Mr. Frog, will you
    give us a song
That's bright and cheery
    and shan't last long?''
Unh-hunh, unh-hunh,
    unh-hunh

''Indeed, Mrs. Mouse,''
    replied the Frog
Unh-hunh, unh-hunh
''Indeed, Mrs. Mouse,''
    replied the Frog
Unh-hunh, unh-hunh
''Indeed, Mrs. Mouse,''
    replied the Frog
''A cold has made me
    hoarse as a hog.''
Unh-hunh, unh-hunh,
    unh-hunh


''Since a cold in the head
    has you laid up
Unh-hunh, unh-hunh

''Since a cold in the head
    has you laid up
Unh-hunh, unh-hunh
''Since a cold in the head
    has you laid up
I'll sing you a song that I
    just made up.''
Unh-hunh, unh-hunh,
    unh-hunh


They all sat down and
    started to chat
Unh-hunh, unh-hunh
They all sat down and
    started to chat
Unh-hunh, unh-hunh

They all sat down and
  started to chat
When in came the kittens
  and the cat
Unh-hunh, unh-hunh,
  unh-hunh

☐

The bride, in fright, she
  runs up the wall
Unh-hunh, unh-hunh
The bride, in fright, she
  runs up the wall
Unh-hunh, unh-hunh
The bride, in fright, she
  runs up the wall
Turns her ankle and down

she falls
Unh-hunh, unh-hunh,
  unh-hunh

☐

They all went a-sailing
  across the lake
Unh-hunh, unh-hunh
They all went a-sailing
  across the lake
Unh-hunh, unh-hunh
They all went a-sailing
  across the  lake
And all got swallowed by a
  big black snake
Unh-hunh, unh-hunh,
  unh-hunh

And the ones who escaped
  were one, two, three
Unh-hunh, unh-hunh
And the ones who escaped
  were one, two, three
Unh-hunh, unh-hunh
And the ones who escaped
  were one, two, three
The Frog, the Rat, and
  Miss Mousie
Unh-hunh, unh-hunh,
  unh-hunh

☐

The Mouse and the Frog
  went off to France
Unh-hunh, unh-hunh

The Mouse and the Frog
    went off to France
Unh-hunh, unh-hunh
The Mouse and the Frog
    went off to France
And that's the end of their
    romance
Unh-hunh, unh-hunh,

unh-hunh

There's bread and jam
    upon the shelf
Unh-hunh, unh-hunh
There's bread and jam

upon the shelf
Unh-hunh, unh-hunh
There's bread and jam
    upon the shelf
If you want some, just help
    yourself
Unh-hunh, unh-hunh,
    unh-hunh

# Rock-A-Bye, Baby

Rock-a-bye, baby
In the tree top
When the wind blows
The cradle will rock
When the bough breaks
The cradle will fall
And down will come Baby
Cradle and all

Baby is drowsing
Cozy and fair
Mother sits near
In her rocking chair

Forward and back
The cradle she swings
And though Baby sleeps
He hears what she sings

From the high rooftops
Down to the sea
No one's as dear
As Baby to me
Wee little fingers
Eyes wide and bright
Now sound asleep
Until morning light

# Oats, Peas, Beans, and Barley Grow

*May be sung as a round.*

Oats, peas, beans, and
  barley grow
Oats, peas, beans, and
  barley grow
Now you nor I nor anyone
  knows
How oats, peas, beans, and
  barley grow

his ease
Stamps his feet and clasps
  his hands
And turns around and sees
  the land

Then the farmer sows his
  seed
Then he stands and takes

Waiting for a partner
Waiting for a partner
Open the ring and bring
  one in
And now we'll gaily dance
  and sing

40

# Pop! Goes the Weasel

All around the cobbler's
    bench
The monkey chased the
    weasel
The monkey said it's all in
    fun

Pop! goes the weasel
A nickel for a spool of thread
A penny for a needle
That's the way the money
    goes
Pop! goes the weasel

# Now We are Gathering Nuts in May

Now we are gathering nuts
  in May
Nuts in May, nuts in May
Now we are gathering nuts
  in May
Out on a frosty morning

□

Who will come over for
  nuts in May
Nuts in May, nuts in
  May
Who will come over for
  nuts in May
Out on a frosty morning?

Sue will come over for nuts
  in May
Nuts in May, nuts in May
Sue will come over for nuts
  in May
Out on a frosty morning

□

Who will come over to

fetch her away
Fetch her away, fetch her
  away
Who will come over to
  fetch her away
Out on a frosty morning?

□

Jack will come over to fetch
  her away
Fetch her away, fetch her
  away
Jack will come over to fetch
  her away
Out on a frosty morning

42

# Lavender's Blue

Lavender's blue, diddle,
   diddle
Lavender's green
When I am King, diddle,
   diddle
You shall be Queen

Call up your men, diddle,
   diddle
Set them to work

Some to the plough,
   diddle, diddle
Some to the cart

Some to make hay, diddle,
   diddle
Some to cut corn
While you and I, diddle,
   diddle
Keep ourselves warm

# This Old Man

This old man, he plays
One.
He plays nick-nack on my
thumb.

With a nick-nack
Paddy-whack
Give the dog a bone
This old man goes rolling
home.

This old man, he plays
Two.

He plays nick-nack on my
shoe.

With a nick-nack
Paddy-whack
Give the dog a bone

This old man goes rolling
home.

This old man, he plays
Three.
He plays nick-nack on my
knee.

With a nick-nack
Paddy-whack
Give the dog a bone
This old man goes rolling
home.

This old man, he plays
    Four.
He plays nick-nack on my
    door.

With a nick-nack
Paddy-whack
Give the dog a bone
This old man goes rolling
    home.

This old man, he plays
    Five.
He plays nick-nack on my
    hive.

With a nick-nack
Paddy-whack
Give the dog a bone
This old man goes rolling
    home.

This old man, he plays Six.
He plays nick-nack on my
    sticks.

With a nick-nack
Paddy-whack
Give the dog a bone
This old man goes rolling
    home.

This old man, he plays
    Seven.
Cross my heart and go to
    Heaven.

With a nick-nack
Paddy-whack
Give the dog a bone
This old man goes rolling
    home.

This old man, he plays
    Eight.
He plays nick-nack on my
    gate.

With a nick-nack
Paddy-whack
Give the dog a bone
This old man goes rolling
    home.

This old man, he plays
    Nine.
He plays nick-nack on my
    twine.

With a nick-nack
Paddy-whack
Give the dog a bone

This old man goes rolling
    home.

This old man, he plays
    Ten.
He plays nick-nack with his
    friends.

With a nick-nack
Paddy-whack
Give the dog a bone
This old man goes rolling
    home.

This old man, he plays
    'Leven.
He plays nick-nack four
    and seven.

With a nick-nack
Paddy-whack
Give the dog a bone
This old man goes rolling
    home.

This old man, he plays
    Twelve.
He plays nick-nack by
    himself.

With a nick-nack
Paddy-whack
Give the dog a bone
This old man goes rolling
  home.

This old man, he plays
  Teens.
He plays nick-nack with

string beans.

With a nick-nack
Paddy-whack
Give the dog a bone
This old man goes rolling
  home.

This old man, he plays

Twenty.
He plays nick-nack on my
  pennies.

With a nick-nack
Paddy-whack
Give the dog a bone
This old man goes rolling
  home.

# Pat-A-Cake

Pat-a-cake pat-a-cake,
  baker's man!
That I will master as quick
  as I can
Prick it and nick it and
  mark it with T

And there will be plenty
  for baby and me
For baby and me, for baby
  and me
And there will be plenty
  for baby and me

# Girls and Boys Come Out to Play

Girls and boys come out to
  play
The moon doth shine as
  bright as day
Come with a whoop and
  come with a call
And come with a good-will
  or not at all
Up the ladder and down
  the wall
A half penny loaf will serve
  us all

Leave your supper and
  leave your sleep
And join your play fellows
  down the street
Come with a whoop and
  come with a call
And come with a good-will
  or not at all
Up the ladder and down
  the wall
A half penny loaf will serve
  us all

# Frère Jacques (Are You Sleeping?)

*May be sung as a round.*

Frère Jacques, Frère Jacques
Dormez-vous? Dormez-
vous?
Sonnez les matines, Sonnez
les matines
Din, din, don! Din, din,
don!

[Traditional English translation:]
Are you sleeping? Are you
sleeping?
Brother John? Brother John?
Morning bells are ringing
Morning bells are ringing
Ding, dong, ding! Ding,
dong, ding!

# The Mulberry Bush

Here we go round the
 Mulberry bush
The Mulberry bush, the
 Mulberry bush
Here we go round the
 Mulberry bush
On a cold and frosty
 morning

This is the way we wash our
 hands
We wash our hands, we
 wash our hands
This is the way we wash our
 hands

On a cold and frosty
 morning

This is the way we dry our
 hands
We dry our hands, we dry
 our hands

This is the way we dry our
 hands
On a cold and frosty
 morning

This is the way we clap our
 hands
We clap our hands, we clap
 our hands
This is the way we clap our
 hands
On a cold and frosty
 morning

This is the way we warm
our hands
We warm our hands, we
warm our hands

This is the way we warm
our hands
On a cold and frosty
morning

# See-Saw Marjorie Daw

See-saw, Marjorie Daw
Jacky shall have a new
master
Jacky shall have but a
penny a day
Because he can't work any
faster

# London Bridge

London Bridge is falling
down
Falling down
Falling down
London Bridge is falling
down
My fair lady

Iron bars will rust and
bend
Rust and bend
Rust and bend
Iron bars will rust and
bend
My brave laddie

Baby's cradle's safe and
sound
Safe and sound
Safe and sound
Baby's cradle's safe and
sound
My brave laddie

Guard it 'round with iron
bars
Iron bars
Iron bars
Guard it 'round with iron
bars
My fair lady

Guard it, then, with
precious gold
Precious gold
Precious gold
Guard it, then, with
precious gold
My fair lady

Precious gold is fare for
  thieves
Fare for thieves
Fare for thieves
Precious gold is fare for
  thieves
My brave laddie

◘

Guard it, then, with
  soldiers strong
Soldiers strong
Soldiers strong
Guard it, then, with
  soldiers strong
My fair lady

Soldiers are all gone to
  war
Gone to war
Gone to war
Soldiers are all gone to
  war
My brave laddie

◘

Guard it, then, with
  watchful love
Watchful love
Watchful love
Guard it, then, with
  watchful love
My fair lady

Baby, then, will sleep all
  night
Sleep all night
Sleep all night
Baby, then, will sleep all
  night
My brave laddie

◘

And she'll grow up straight
  and tall
Straight and tall
Straight and tall
And she'll grow up straight
  and tall
My fair lady

# I Had a Little Nut Tree

I had a little nut tree
Nothing would it bear
But a silver nutmeg
And a golden pear

The King of Spain's daughter
Came to visit me
And all for the sake of my
little nut tree

# Alphabet Song

A, B, C, D, E, F, G,
H, I, J, K, L, M, N, O, P.
Q, R, S, T, U and V,
W, X and Y and Z.
Now I know my ABCs
Next time won't you sing
with me?

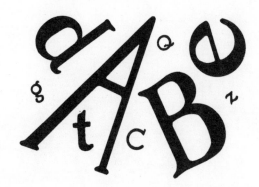

# Lazy Sheep, Pray Tell Me Why?

Lazy sheep, pray tell me
    why
In the pleasant field you lie
Eating grass and daisies
    white
From the morning till the
    night?
Ev'rything can something do
But what kind of use are
    you?

"Nay, my little master, nay
Do not serve me so, I pray
Don't you see the wool
    that grows
On the back to make your
    clothes?
Cold, ah, very cold you'd
    be
If you had not wool from
    me."

# The Spider and the Fly

"Will you walk into my
parlor?" said the spider
to the fly
"'Tis the prettiest little
parlor that ever you
did spy
The way into my parlor is
up a winding stair
And I have many pretty
things to show you when
you're there."
"Oh, no, no!" said the
little fly, "To ask me
is in vain
For who goes up your

winding stair, shall ne'er
come down again."

"I am sure you must be
weary, dear! with soaring
up so high

Will you rest upon my
little bed?" said the
spider to the fly
"There are pretty curtains
drawn around, the sheets
are fine and thin
And if you like to rest
awhile, I'll snugly tuck
you in."
"Oh, no, no!" said the
little fly, "For I have
heard it said
They never, never wake
again who sleep upon
your bed."

The spider turned him round about and went into his den
For well he knew the silly fly would soon come back again
So he wove a subtle web in a little corner sly
And he set his table ready to dine upon the fly
Then he came out to his door again and merrily did sing
"Come hither, hither, pretty fly with the pearl and silver wing."

Alas! alas! how very soon this silly little fly
Hearing all these flattering speeches came quickly buzzing by

With gauzy wing she hung aloft, then near and nearer drew
Thinking only of her crested head and gold and purple hue
Thinking only of her brilliant wings poor silly thing, at last
Up jumped the wicked spider and fiercely held her fast!

# Did You Ever See a Lassie?

Did you ever see a lassie,
  a lassie, a lassie
Did you ever see a lassie go
  this way then that?

Go this way then that way,
  then this way then that way
Did you ever see a lassie go
  this way then that?

# Skip to My Lou

Skip, skip, skip to my Lou
Skip, skip, skip to my Lou
Skip, skip, skip to my Lou
Skip to my Lou, my
    darling!

Lost my partner, what'll I
    do?
Lost my partner, what'll I
    do?
Lost my partner, what'll I
    do?
Skip to my Lou, my
    darling!

Skip, skip, skip to my Lou
Skip, skip, skip to my Lou
Skip, skip, skip to my Lou
Skip to my Lou, my
    darling!

I'll get another one, better
    than you

I'll get another one, better
    than you
. I'll get another one, better
    than you
Skip to my Lou, my
    darling!
Skip, skip, skip to my Lou
Skip, skip, skip to my Lou
Skip, skip, skip to my Lou
Skip to my Lou, my
    darling!

Flies in the sugar bowl,

shoo, fly, shoo
Flies in the sugar bowl,
   shoo, fly, shoo
Flies in the sugar bowl,
   shoo, fly, shoo
Skip to my Lou, my
   darling!

Skip, skip, skip to my Lou
Skip, skip, skip to my Lou
Skip, skip, skip to my Lou
Skip to my Lou, my
   darling!

Mice in the cupboard,
   what'll I do

Mice in the cupboard,
   what'll I do
Mice in the cupboard,
   what'll I do
Skip to my Lou, my
   darling!

Skip, skip, skip to my Lou
Skip, skip, skip to my Lou
Skip, skip, skip to my Lou
Skip to my Lou, my
   darling!

Birds on the rooftop, red
   and blue
Birds on the rooftop, red

and blue
Birds on the rooftop, red
   and blue
Skip to my Lou, my
   darling!

Skip, skip, skip to my Lou
Skip, skip, skip to my Lou
Skip, skip, skip to my Lou
Skip to my Lou, my
   darling!

Cows in the pasture, moo,
   moo, moo
Cows in the pasture, moo,
   moo, moo

Cows in the pasture, moo,
   moo, moo
Skip to my Lou, my
   darling!

Skip, skip, skip to my Lou

Skip, skip, skip to my Lou
Skip, skip, skip to my Lou
Skip to my Lou, my
   darling!

Dogs in the hayfield, two

by two
Dogs in the hayfield, two
   by two
Dogs in the hayfield, two
   by two
Skip to my Lou, my
   darling!

# Row, Row, Row Your Boat

*May be sung as a round.*

Row, row, row your boat
Gently down the stream
Merrily, merrily, merrily,
   merrily
Life is but a dream

# Polly Put the Kettle On

Polly put the kettle on,
    Polly put the kettle on
Polly put the kettle on,
    we'll all have tea

Sukey take it off again,
    Sukey take it off again
Sukey take it off again,
    they've all gone away